The Farewell Tourist

THE FAREWELL TOURIST

Alison Glenny

OTAGO UNIVERSITY PRESS

To the memory of my mother and father, and the dogs

Contents

THE MAGNETIC PROCESS

I

She would wait for him in the morning room, seated on a velvet sofa. Each time he visited she was delighted when he produced a bouquet of flowers, summoned out of thin air. He spoke of his belief that materials absorb the identity of those who handle them. Sometimes their fingers would touch during the examination of an object. The inevitable sparks were part of what he called *the magnetic process.*

II

He considered her body to be a little machine, remarkable for its feats of transmission. Encouraged to speak into the trumpet, she was startled to hear her voice emerge as clicks, groans, and a strange whistling sound. She pretended to be the wind, and he enacted a magnetic storm around her. In the final act, she helped him demonstrate the tent. Emerging over and over from the triangle of canvas, each time to fresh applause.

III

The little book, he said, had gone all the way to
Antarctica, and he insisted on her keeping it next to her
bed. She would sometimes take it out and turn the pages,
searching for hints of its experience. To her disap-
pointment, its pages showed no signs of alteration.
One day she left it behind by accident while stepping
down from a bus. It had gone off, she told him, in search
of new adventures. Not admitting the relief she felt to
wake in the morning and not be greeted by its poker face,
its obdurate blankness.

IV

Growing up in a house filled with harps and bicycles, he pursued nature with nets, a light trap, and a killing bottle. For an entire year he walked around with a telescope permanently fixed to one eye. He enjoyed the way it made the world vanish and brought another one into view. His brothers and sisters were planets and moons, orbiting each other in complicated ellipses. Sometimes their movements grew agitated. When his sister broke his telescope, he cried and sulked for days. Grieving for the boy who had been lost in the middle distance, a disembodied presence with a curious eye.

V

The piano was an essential tool of polar exploration, yet they struggled to fit all its pieces together. Part of the interior was found to be missing, and they thought it might be in the crate that had fallen to the bottom of the bay. An hour of dredging uncovered a box that was winched to the surface but contained only a tide gauge and an instrument for measuring wind chill. Eventually they abandoned it on the ice. Once, it was inspected by a penguin, which was captured and skinned. Watching the case sink into the ice, they argued about the fugue. The geologist described it as the highest achievement of counterpoint. The doctor disagreed. The fugue, he insisted, was a disorder characterised by memory-loss and travel.

VI

Each morning she descended into the ice pit to take the measurements, working her way down through the strata. Pushing the thermometer into the white wall, weighing the little bags with their samples of snow. The pencil served both to measure firmness and to enter the observations. Coming indoors she shed cold as vapour; a tiny fumerole. Stamping her feet, bending down to brush the snow from the toes of her narrow boots.

VII

He called it *the little observatory*. The instrument, he explained, was used for measuring the electrical state of the atmosphere. The wooden box, with the latch that was too small to be opened by a mittened hand. Later, the photographer disappeared into a bag with only his arms showing. Darkness was necessary, he explained, if you wanted to capture light.

VIII

She was finding it difficult to leave the house without
taking the glossopteris in its bed of rock. In the waiting
room she felt its small weight press against her thigh. The
patient before her had a face permanently frozen in a gesture
of alarm. When it was her turn she told the doctor of her
predicament. The sudden freezing spells, the fits of
shuddering, and their opposite – moments when she was
flooded with light, a camera lens at the moment the
aperture opens. He told her she was *having difficulty seeing
around the object* and asked her *did she ever dream of snow.*

IX

He dreamed of a device that would shrink the landscape so it could be scooped up by hand and examined through a jeweller's glass. Its features minutely surveyed without leaving the warmth of his sleeping bag. Outside, the mountains were buried to their necks. Icebergs hung upside down in the sky. He noted that *everything about conventional perspective is violated.* The doctor cut open the stomach of a penguin but discovered only a few stones and a cuttlefish beak.

X

She dreamed she was on a ship that was sinking. She could
see the gleaming surface of the iceberg, feel the cold water
rise above her ankles. But she was seated with the violins
and preoccupied by details; the amount of rosin on her bow,
a false note from the woodwind, and the frayed portion of
sleeve at her wrist – did it show? The damp patches in the
conductor's armpits as he raised his arms to draw out the
rising swell of sound. The luminous points of his white collar.
On waking, she asked herself why she didn't try to reach the
lifeboats. Her friend told her the answer, *you didn't want to
interrupt the music.*

XI

It was elusive and it wandered, so they thought of it as female. It attracted them the way the oceans are tugged by the moon, and in surrendering to its pull, they knew themselves to be men. It helped that it was always day. Loading and unloading the sledges he counted off each item: trail flags, primus box, special Navy biscuits, the small pannikin for travelling. The photograph in his breast pocket reminded him of the time when he did his exploring mostly by touch. Sometimes the moon shone through the thin curtains. It helped to fix his image in her mind, she said. Before a continent grew between them, and he could no longer resist its magnetic attraction.

XII

Some afternoons a fog rolled down the hallway. On others, the staircase groaned with moisture. A finger laid carelessly on a bannister dislodged a ledge of rime. She lifted the hem of her dress to avoid the damp in the passageway, wore knitted gloves in the kitchen. She was lying in the bath when the glacier pushed through the wall. She sank deeper into the water to escape the chill that settled on her shoulders. Trying to ignore the white haze, to lose herself between the pages of her book.

XIII

They referred to it as *the dainty food*. A small stick of
chocolate, the queer taste of a cigarette. Helge was a
different matter, but by the time they had finished there
was nothing left but his teeth and the tuft at the end of his
tail. They spoke of a fat Polar hoosh. Of the time when each
day brought a surprise in the form of a new omelette or a
fine cake. Recalling how the cook would say 'I'm going out
to kill the dinner,' as he pushed the door open with the toe
of his boot.

XIV

At the bottom of the garden she used a stick to draw lines
on the ground to represent the geologic eras. The oldest
jumped straight to the Holocene and demanded to know
what came next. The baby tripped and fell in the
Cretaceous, tore his blouse, and had to be picked up and
comforted. She sat up mending the tear by lamplight.
Tying the tiny knot, biting the thread between her teeth. As
the cold settled around her shoulders she imagined herself
on the ice shelf, fashioning a needle from the wing bone of
a shearwater. Watching the light as it refused to fade,
waiting for one era to change into another.

XV

He noted that *the rapid closing of the season is ominous.*
They hung up their clothes by spitting on them and
pressing them to the wall. The decision to abandon the
theodolite was not easily made, but seemed inevitable. In
his dreams food was continually being offered and then
whisked away, often on the flimsiest of pretences. Waking,
he trudged outside to take the measurements. Crouching
in front of the wooden box with its louvred sides enclosing
the thermometer. On the way back he poled the snow for
hidden crevasses. Slits or fissures with unfathomable
depths, holding azure light.

XVI

Some nights the staircase disappeared and was replaced by an ice tongue. She improvised crampons using nails, spiked boots to descend the slick surface. In the morning the house was back to rights, although at moments the night would impose itself unexpectedly. Gazing at the hinge of her jewellery box, for example, she would be seized by a sudden vertigo. Overtaken by a conviction that the dressing table, room, and everything in it had detached from the house and was floating away, calving new impossibilities as it drifted from the dynamic boundary.

XVII

He wrote of his interest in the forms of the ice. Of the most delicate crystals that withered at a breath, and needed to be photographed in situ. How there was no possibility of bringing back specimens for study in the hut during the dark months. Watching the photographer at work, he recalled his own amateur attempts. Her pale torso rising from the crumpled drapery. At the last minute he'd scooped a handful of snow from a branch to clean the nitrate from his fingers. In his hurry to expose the plate he'd dropped it, felt it slip from between his hands and shatter on the ground.

XVIII

She was retreating. But was it possible to avoid
vanishing altogether, a committed retreat? She recalled
how he would sometimes refer to the grounding line. How
she once misheard it as 'drowning'. When the forcing
starts, he said, it can't be stopped but goes faster and
faster. Take this bed for example, its zones of divergence.
The ice pillow and the continents beneath, hidden from
sight. Her friends told her *it will be fine, as long as you
don't run away*. But she could feel herself gaining speed, a
fierce momentum. As if, before long, nothing could hold
her back.

XIX

Some days he seemed to fade almost to nothing. The
photographs showed a stranger, a silvery absence that
highlighted the small marks of mould or discoloration.
The mole above his eyebrow, for instance. Had it always
been there, or was it a later addition? Sometimes a
creaking stair would make her turn, or she'd glimpse a
figure dart into the shadows behind the door. Eventually,
even the ghosts would depart. The pictures would walk out
of their frames and disappear, leaving only a vacancy and
a scattering of loose snow.

DRIFT

(verb)

1. To collect in heaps driven together by the wind. *Snow had drifted deep over the path.* 2. To move or pass passively or aimlessly; to wander. 3. To be carried away by a current of air or water.
4. To cover with drifts of snow. 5. To drive at, aim at, try to effect.
6. To put off, delay, defer. 7. To accumulate meaning, as snow accumulates. 8. Of a man or woman, gradually to lose mutual affection.

(noun)

1. A continuous slow movement from one place to another. 2. An accumulation of snow or sand driven together by the wind. *A drift of lovely lace fell over her large sleeves.* 3. The general intention or meaning of an argument or someone's remarks. 4. The influence of wind currents on the migration of birds. *Deviation from the direct route is mainly due to drift.* 5. In architecture, the horizontal thrust of an arch. 6. The deviation of a ship from its course. 7. A slow variation in the characteristics or operation of an electrical circuit or device. 8. A group of stars having a random distribution of velocities but with an apparent motion towards some point in the sky. 9. A scheme, plot, design, or device. 10. A characteristic of journeys in regions where the compass proves unreliable, as in proximity to the magnetic pole. 11. The gradual unravelling of a vow or promise.

Footnotes to The Heroic Age

---

1   He declared his intention of taking the ponies, five dozen sled dogs, and 'a motor car for use wherever there are no mountains'.

2   Each of his letters was a tiny museum, a footnote to an imaginary novel. 'I searched the box of negatives to discover the keepsakes, but they had vanished in the silence of the crevasses.'

3   Despite their efforts, the snow came inside. Each day they used the wing of a giant storm petrel to sweep it out again.

4   She had placed the instrument in the snow outside her bedroom window. The crossed lenses revealed the inner stress, the point of inevitable fracture.

5   He reported that the cold affected the delicate workings of the clockwork. 'Each morning I spend an hour regulating and winding my chronometer.'

6   The absence of daylight was partly compensated for by an excellent little blubber lamp, which burned with a clear white flame.

7   She dreamed that winter was a little cabinet. When she unlocked it, she discovered a small white dog.

8 *The age of averted interest*
   Late afternoons were characterised by ennui, described as
   'a veil of indifferent sensations'. There was an increase in
   compositions for solo piano, and sailing ships were largely
   replaced by toys made of balsa and canvas, launched by
   children on unmanned explorations of ponds and streams.

9 'My poor pen is powerless to describe [--].'

10 Overnight the medical brandy froze solid and a bottle of
   champagne splintered. The liquid formed stalactites, which they
   broke off and ate.

11 'In the darkroom I hold my breath to prevent a fine snow from
   covering the surface of the plates.'

¹² Reported phenomena included a feeling of being watched, and hearing a voice on the stairs. 'Whenever I entered a room, the sound of ice splintering and a sensation of avalanches.'

¹³ *Apport*

    1. Production of an object, supposedly by occult means.
    2. The object so produced.
    3. (*obsolete*) Bearing, port.

The first session. A soft ethereal light played above a woman's head. The hostess reported the sensation of a cold hand on her neck.

The second session. 'The curtains were drawn, and the lamps extinguished. In the darkness they distinctly heard the ticking of a clock, the gentle whirr of a motor, and the trembling note of an electric bell.'

14 He wrote to say that he was vanishing for a time into the unknown, but would return with a sledge full of scientific curiosities and observations. Despite the faithfulness of the machine, the effortless whirring of its gears, she clung to this belief.

15 On a shelf inside the door of the hut, they found a windproof mitten filled with nails.

16 *Blizzard*
    1. A severe snowstorm with high winds.
    2. A large or overwhelming number of things occuring suddenly.

17 The cinematograph film showed a man emerging from a tent and disappearing. At that point the images ceased and the only sound was the whirring of the projector.

Footnotes to a History of the Atmosphere

---

1   *Atlas des Nuages*. Known in English as *Vincent's Cloud Atlas*. The chromolithographs were the inspiration for her twenty-four watercolour paintings of clouds.

2   The novel, which was never completed, depicts a woman attempting to write a a history of metereology while moving through a series of public assemblies and ballrooms ventilated by the use of ice.

3   *Illuminance*

        Total luminous flux received on the unit area of a surface. Typically expressed in measurements such as the *phot, lux,* and *foot-candle.* Cf *penumbra, transit.*

4   As they travelled deeper into the mountains, it became harder to
    discover the dew point. She noted the 'uncomfortable diffused
    light', and that blindness was caused by gazing too long through
    the instruments.

5   A reference to her dissertation, which she had planned to write on
    the three kinds of twilight.

6   To pursue the anomaly to a definite conclusion would have
    required following the clouds into the upper atmosphere, where
    they die as they rise into the cold thin air.

7   'I had wanted to describe the atmosphere, its subtle architecture.
    But the unreliability of the instruments affected the quality of the
    observations. Instead of the clicking of gears, an ominous silence.'

[8] A small pocket spectroscope. 'I used it to determine the luminosity of the object, and whether the source of the illumination was moonlight or the dawn.'

[9] He wrote to express his delight with the photographs. In the absence of a prism to filter polarised light, she had used mirrors and lake surfaces to capture the clouds.

[10] The film, designed to be screened through a piece of blue glass, recounts a young woman's growing obsession with a scientific instrument. Audiences were shocked by the suggestion that the illicit passion had been sanctioned by her governess.

[11] She noted that his visits seemed to take place *elsewhere*. 'The ice-covered chalet for example, or the hut used for the weather observations.'

Draperies

Described as 'the most novel and delicious mode of decorating a ballroom'. The most popular colour was the shade of purple known as *Lumiere etiquette violette*. Cyan and a pale apple green were also much admired.

Pulsating arcs

She noted that the effect, which was obtained by the use of a small machine concealed behind a folding screen, seldom failed to elicit expressions of astonishment.

Feeble glow

The least of the decorations. Sometimes confused with the first appearance of dawn, or a fire observed at a distance.

[13]   She concluded that a region around the earth is 'forbidden' to the solar stream. It did not explain the letters that continued to arrive from Norway, or the gifts of ice and preserved pears.

[14]   Strictly speaking, it was impossible to determine the amount of condensation. She spoke mainly of a feeling of heaviness, which appeared to be related to the weight of the impressions.

[15]   A reference to the invention of the electrical chandelier, said to be the result of the Emperor's fear of gaslight. The crystal finials allude to the redundant candles, but did not prevent the disastrous fire of 1883 that destroyed the ballroom.

Footnotes to A History of the Cryosphere

---

1. *Études sur les glaciers.* A pencilled note in the margin conveyed her sudden sense of being in the wrong place and the wrong time. 'As if I had been a part of something then abandoned.'

2. By the time they reached the second hotel, they were deep in winter. The word 'bewitched' might have been ominous, but instead seemed to convey an enchantment effected by snow, moonlight, and the slender avenue lined with trees.

3. A reference to her little adze pick, which she used to reveal a fragment of the truth.

4   Every few months an envelope arrived enclosing fresh drawings of
    snowflakes. She was unsure whether to interpret the gifts as a form
    of courtship.

5   In the novel the heroine, who is dying of consumption, complains
    of having 'a whole winter of ice on my chest'. Critics note that the
    practice of cooling drinks with ice or snow was not introduced to
    Europe until the seventeenth century, when it was adopted only
    by persons of great refinement.

6   The scene in which the Duke escorts her on a tour of his estate,
    culminating in a visit to the ice conservatory. 'The sensation of
    coldness, intially welcome after the fierce heat of the sun, was
    gradually replaced by a deeper chill, like a prolonged internal
    shudder.'

[7] *Erratic*

From Latin *errare*, to wander. Irregular or eccentric in conduct, habit or opinion. *The huge erratics of the late cold period.*

[8] The theory originated in her observation of the behaviour of the vapour escaping when a champagne bottle is uncorked; in her memoir she refers to the phenomenon as a form of frost smoke.

[9] *Ice hour*

1. Mean interval between the culmination of the moon and the closest following tidal compression of ice at any given point. Used by navigators for plotting courses, and planning the arrival and departure time of vessels.

2. Russian silent-era film in which the heroine embarks on an affair with an Arctic explorer. In her memoir, she likens her pursuit of this obscure masterpiece to an 'obsession'.

10   *Embacle*

Literally, the heaping up of ice that follows a renewed freezing. In the correspondence, the term they used to refer to any unexpected obstacle that prevented them from keeping an assignation.

11   *Freezing point*

'I had simply reached an impasse in life where it was no longer possible to go forward, yet retreat was equally impossible.'

12   *Metamorphosis*

In his farewell letter, he regretted their 'continuous state of transformation'. This letter, together with the photograph of the hermitage, formed the basis of the episode in her experimental novel in which the heroine covers herself in pieces of torn paper.

13   The album containing seventy-six photographs of snow, one for every day of their affair. 'The envelopes continued to arrive, filled only with silence, but curiously heavy.'

FOOTNOTES TO A HISTORY OF THE HONEYMOON

---

[1] Referred to by the French as *Voyage à la façon anglaise*. Histories of the Belle Époque refer to it as the first instance of modern mass tourism.

[2] 'The black chiffon nightgown that, impulsively, I had bought in Chile, but never wore.'

[3] He described it in his letters as the month in which 'there is nothing but tenderness and pleasure'. She preferred the explanation that it originally referred to the inevitable waning of love, like a phase of the moon.

4   While leafing through the uncorrected pages she was surprised by their unexpected energy and force. This led to her attempts to reassemble the romance.

5   The choice of a white wedding dress, said to have begun the fashion among naval officers of travelling to Antarctica for their honeymoon.

6   In a letter to her sister-in-law she complained about his 'swift and frigid visits'. His account, written several years later, referred to their honeymoon as 'The Great Cooling'.

7   Reportedly, the first wedding to introduce choral music to the processional. Not to be confused with *mariage blanc*, 'silence and mist and vague terrors'.

Corsage
   1. The bodice of a woman's dress.
   2. The body of a bird, excluding its wings.
   3. A small bouquet worn on the dress or wrist. *She had bought the corsage of forget-me-nots herself, explaining that gardenias gave her a headache.*

9 During the ceremony he filled a box with snow to see the effect of time on it. Elsewhere she reports that 'the men did detailed domestic chores with feminine precision'.

10 Among the gifts were several fine specimens of ventrolite, and a lunar meteorite. Afterwards several of the guests were observed pushing a block of ice through the streets.

11 'I tried to repeat the vows, but I no longer recognised my own voice, while my fingers had become frozen to the bouquet –'

12 'Following the dream's recurrence over several nights, I realised that the vistas of ice shelves and glaciers referred to the wedding cake, or was it the other way around?'

13 Conventionally, the first journey of a ship or passenger. Also used colloquially to refer to a period of prolonged or focussed attention that culminates in a sea voyage.

14 Recurring images included the shattered plates, an envelope filled with snow, a wedding dress that was too heavy or damaged by moths, and the row of tiny boxes, each one with its hasp frozen shut.

Footnotes to A History of Climate

1   The title of her first book of poems, sometimes credited with
    inaugurating the genre of 'ice melancholy'.

2   The phenomon of luxury cruises – increasingly fashionable as
    the century progressed – that took tourists to view the icebergs
    at close quarters as they drifted north. Regarded as a form
    of 'farewell tourism', they were renowned for their elaborate
    entertainments and lavish menus.

3   A small room contained the weather diaries. White cotton gloves
    were arranged on the tables. It was noted that at one time entire
    cities were illuminated by whales.

[4]   *Eccentricity.* It took an increasing effort to maintain a regular course. Her entire routine seemed to have grown flatter and more elongated, as if she were drawn to the colder and less populated regions of the spaces she entered.

Obliquity. She recalled her mother's fondness for hats; her habit of tilting her head to one side, like a bird.

Precession. Each year the sun seemed to take longer to climb the sky. As if the seasons were slipping backward, rather than moving forward.

[5]   For her first exhibition she filled the gallery with spheres. Also a lake with a dark surface in which visitors were invited to view a reflection of their internal weather.

6   The Museum of the Vanishing World is itself disappearing, piece by piece. Visitors note that between one visit and another a wall will have vanished, or a staircase disappeared, making orderly progress through the different parts of the collection difficult, if not impossible. Cf *trophic cascade.*

7   Throughout the exhibition the symbol of a dagger (†) next to the species name is typically used to indicate that the last remaining member has died.

8   Refers to her history of the buttonhole. She explains that this mode of fastening is believed to have been invented during the Little Ice Age, together with the knitted undergarment.

9   The machine had a handle that visitors were invited to turn, releasing steam into the air. The label described it as a 'practical demonstration of the human domination of climate'.

[10] The book in which he predicted the replacement of the museum by aquaria. It included drawings of bathyspheres, operated by mechanical oars, that would assist visitors to move between the exhibits.

[11] 'In an attempt to capture the emotions of the early days of my marriage, I returned to the valley where we had spent our honeymoon. We had chosen the hotel because of its location at the foot of a glacier. Since then, the glacier had retreated. The rooms, with their decorations of antlers and hunting rifles, were the same, only slightly shabbier. I slept poorly, kept awake by the sound of the machines used to manufacture snow.'

[12] In the memoir he noted that the relics, never exhibited, included the melancholy candles of evening, the notorious dream of the chandelier, and the photograph of glaciers moving their tongues in the sea.

[13] Referring to a promenade and venue dedicated to transitory entertainments. Traditionally regarded as a symbol of mutability and loss. See also *Frost Fair*.

Appendix 1

Magnetic Traces

Erasure

1. An act or instance of erasing. 2. The removal of all traces of something: obliteration. 3. The state of having been erased; total blankness. 4. The place or mark, as on a piece of paper, where something has been erased. *There were several erasures on the paper.* 5. Crossing out, striking out, blotting out, effacement, expunging. 6. A tendency to ignore or conceal an element of society. 7. Removal of something in order to reveal another: for example, the discovery that the beloved has been replaced by a set of measurements.
8. The practice of concealing part of a poem by covering it with snow.

Her

velvet

~~bouquet~~

~~their~~ fingers

magnetic.

She would   turn ~~the pages~~

wake in

blankness

A telescope

                    orbiting

        his sister's

                    ~~disembodied~~

eye

The

    ~~small~~ weight

                     of her

predicament

flooded with ~~light~~

    ~~and~~   snow

A   landscape

~~buried~~

in the sky

everything

cut open

Gleaming

water

the violin's

false note.

Afternoons

        dislodged a

            chill

             ~~white haze~~.

~~Ominous~~

dreams

~~measurements~~

enclosing

hidden

light.

A

~~possibility of~~

dark months

~~fingers~~

slip   and

shatter.

A

creaking

door

ghosts

scattering ~~snow~~

Appendix 2

Correspondence

~~Dearest~~

~~A year today since you left, and I thought of you as I walked~~
~~through the empty rooms. Wishing that a bridge might~~
~~appear or a door open so I could step through to wherever~~
~~you are.~~ If I half close my eyes, the shadows seem more solid
and I can almost imagine you are beside me. Before going to
bed I sit in front of the mirror in the hope that it will make me
feel less alone. I pretend that you are standing behind me and
that you are unfastening the clasp of my necklace. ~~Gazing into~~
~~the mirror, I wait for you to lean forward and blow out the~~
~~candle —~~

~~This is to tell you I am sorry. For everything: the oceans, the birds, the invertebrates.~~ Today, watching the wind unlatch the leaves and tumble them in piles, I reminded myself this is a natural process and should not be a cause of sorrow. But what about when the seasons change forever? ~~When spring arrives earlier and autumn later, or not at all.~~ When summer is a record only of melting, and each winter extinguishes the memory of the one that precedes it –?

My dear

Your little pillows are appreciated also the pipes

[*Bottom of page torn off and missing*]

There will be no one who does such beautiful maps as you

[*The remainder of the letter is crossed out*]

You must not give way to despondency

[*The remainder of the paper is torn off and missing*]

Do not let the weather do not

[*The remainder of the sentence is illegible*]

One of my little notes will surely reach you

[*Lines torn off and missing*]

You are twisted into my being

[The remainder of the letter is missing]

ACKNOWLEDGEMENTS

Even a small book incurs large debts of gratitude. Without the generosity of Bill Manhire and the Kathleen Grattan Estate and Trustees, this book would not exist. My thanks also to Bill for valuable suggestions on the manuscript. Thanks to Mark Williams, Lynn Jenner, the University of Canterbury, and Gateway Antarctica, which administers the Postgraduate Certificate in Antarctic Studies. Special thanks to my fellow students from PCAS 2016/17 and to Daniela Liggett, Patrick Shepherd, and Bernadette Hall. My thanks to Antarctica New Zealand and the staff of Scott Base for hospitality and support in Antarctica, and to David Glenny for having me to stay in Christchurch. Thanks to Reuben Bryant and Elizabeth Perkins for valued technical support, to Reid Perkins for enduring friendship and mix-tapes, and to Rachel O'Neill (first responder) for your example and optimism, for supporting my ice obsession, and encouraging me to post the manuscript. And my thanks to Rachel Scott, Fiona Moffat, Imogen Coxhead, and all at Otago University Press for turning it into the book you are holding. Me te aroha nui ki a koutou katoa.

Sources

Page 13: the reference to the piano as 'an essential tool of polar exploration' is from *Antarctica: Music, sounds, and cultural connections* by Bernadette Hince, Rupert Summerson and Arnan Wiesel, Acton, NSW: ANU Press, 2015.

Page 21: 'A small stick of chocolate', 'the queer taste of a cigarette' and 'a fat Polar hoosh' are from *Journals: Captain Scott's last expedition* (Oxford University Press, 2006). The description of eating Helge is from Roald Amundsen, *The South Pole: An account of the Norwegian antarctic expedition in the 'Fram', 1910–1912*, London: J. Murray, 1912.

Page 23: 'the rapid closing of the season is ominous' is from *Journals: Captain Scott's last expedition.*

Page 33: 'Each morning I spend an hour regulating and winding my chronometer' is from *The Shackleton Letters: Behind the scenes of the Nimrod Expedition.*

Page 43: the phrase 'a whole winter of ice on my chest' is from *The Lady of the Camellias (La Dame aux camélias)* by Alexandre Dumas, fils (1848). Information on the history of using ice to cool drinks and ventilate ballrooms is from *Harvest of the Cold Months: The social history of ice and ices* by Elizabeth David, London: M. Joseph, 1994.

Pages 46 and 48: 'The black chiffon nightgown …' and 'the men did detailed domestic chores …' are from *My Antarctic Honeymoon: A Year at the bottom of the world* by Jennie Darlington (as told to Jane McIlvaine), London: Frederick Muller, 1957.

Appendix 2: Correspondence: Fragments are taken from *The Shackleton Letters: Behind the scenes of the Nimrod Expedition* by Regina W Daly (ed.), Norwich: Erskine Press, 2009.

Page 76: 'One of my little notes will surely reach you' is from a letter by Edward Wilson to Oriana Wilson, in *Edward Wilson of the Antarctic: Naturalist and friend* by George Seaver, London: John Murray, 1938 (1933).

Published by Otago University Press
Level 1, 398 Cumberland Street
Dunedin, New Zealand
university.press@otago.ac.nz
www.otago.ac.nz/press

First published 2018

ISBN 978-1-98-853129-8

Design/layout: Fiona Moffat

Front cover: Adapted detail from Herbert Ponting, 'Ice-Blink over the Barrier. Jan 3rd 1911'. Ref P2005/5/105. Scott Polar Research Institute, University of Cambridge, with permission.

Printed in New Zealand by Southern Colour Print, Dunedin.